ZEN DOG

Photographs by Toni Tucker

Concept by Judith Adler

CLARKSON POTTER/PUBLISHERS

NEW YORK

Published by Clarkson Potter/Publishers, New York, New York.
Member of the Crown Publishing Group.

Random House, Inc. New York, Toronto, London, Sydney, Auckland
www.randomhouse.com

CLARKSON N. POTTER is a trademark and POTTER
and colophon are registered trademarks of Random House, Inc.

Printed in China

Design by Lisa Sloane

Library of Congress Cataloging-in-Publication Data
Tucker, Toni.
Zen dog / by Toni Tucker and Judith Adler.
1. Dogs.   2. Dogs—Religious aspects.   3. Zen Buddhism—Quotations, maxims, etc.
I. Adler, Judith.   II. Title.
SF426.2.A34   2001
636.7—dc21   00-069223

ISBN 0-609-60879-7

10 9 8 7 6 5 4 3 2

To my youngest beloveds: Nicky, Will, and Mac.
And to my wondrous bichons who fill my life with love and joy. —T.T.

To all the dogs I've loved before . . .
who've traveled in and out (and in and out, and in and out) my door . . .
And to the Zen-est of them all, my beloved magic Pele. —J.A.

ACKNOWLEDGMENTS

First and foremost, we wish to thank all the dogs who have taught us so many Zen lessons in this life. We offer our heartfelt thanks to these wise counselors who have been there for us every step of the way, teaching us to sit, stay, and heel at just the right times.

Thanks to all of our *Zen Dog* models; to Sara Gregware at the Canine Sports Center in Goshen, Connecticut, who helped us find each other; and to the Little Guild of St. Francis in West Cornwall, Connecticut, for their generous hospitality.

Many thanks to our literary agent, Susan Golomb (and, of course, Kara), for her support and enthusiasm from the very beginning. And to Robert, for being the calm Zen voice of reason, a special thank you.

Our gratitude goes to Margot Schupf, for her kindness and patience with our beginners' minds as we pawed our way through the editorial process of getting *Zen Dog* to bark up the right tree, and to all the folks at Clarkson Potter: Marysarah Quinn, Maggie Hinders, Liana Faughnan, and Joy Sikorski. Thanks also to designer Lisa Sloane.

We are also grateful to our many teachers who have guided us in our journeys, especially our friends and family who journeyed right along with us, offering gentle pats on the head and kind words at just the right moments. Thank you, and please consider this a loving wag of gratitude and appreciation.

STUDENT
How can I find my Buddha nature?

TEACHER
You have no Buddha nature.

STUDENT
What about dogs?

TEACHER
They do have Buddha nature.

STUDENT
Then why do I not have Buddha nature?

TEACHER
Because you have to ask.

D ogs don't simply have Buddha nature: Their very dogginess *is* Buddha nature. And what makes dogs the furry, slobbering, bark-ing, begging, shedding little *Zen* masters that they are? Well, there's a koan, or Buddhist saying, from twentieth-century Zen master Shunryu Suzuki that sums it up nicely: There is something blasphemous in talking about how Buddhism is perfect as a philosophy or teaching without knowing what it actually is. We couldn't agree more. We'd never presume to presume we know. And neither would a dog. And *that* is exactly the tree *Zen Dog* is barking up. Even on the doggiest of days, dogs sit, stay, and wag devotion, hon-esty, loyalty, love, compassion, and joy, the purest of Zen qualities. It's as plain as the cold, wet noses on their faces. Canines are in the moment. Every minute, beginning and ending with the next stick, ball, table scrap, or really stinky smell they can sniff out, dogs live the true joy of life.

Surely it's no accident dogs were the first animals domesticated by man, and they've been loyal ever since. Maybe that's why they're so sure they belong on the bed—thousands of years of service ought to be worth at least one good night's sleep. And after a lousy day at work, those pure, sweet, puppy-dog eyes, gazing up at you with dogged devotion, melt away even the toughest stress and saddest of spirits. And when spirits are high, dogs will do most anything to share in the happiness, bound-ing with positive energy, wagging their entire bodies, and jumping for joy, specifi-cally yours.

Maybe a single dog year is worth seven human years because dogs don't have useless things hanging in their minds and can instead squeeze in seven times more love in a year than any of us ever could. In the no–accounting–for–taste category, dogs win big time. How often have you seen dogs unconditionally love their people, even the most difficult ones, in ways it would seem Buddha himself would have a challenge mastering. Perhaps they love such challenging people simply because they can, volunteering for emotional combat duty because they know, as Buddha did, that hate is not conquered by hate, hate is conquered by love. Loyal dogs teach their people, even "non–people" people, how to love in new and different ways.

Another gift canines bring to our lives is a lesson in the art of mastering the truly important—an afternoon nap in a patch of sunshine, a game of catch on a glorious spring day, or a nice long walk to nowhere. We learn patience when we try to teach them to master the art of sitting, staying, or fetching. Anyone who's been barked awake at dawn and begged for a walk has had a lesson in selfless devotion. Kind of makes you wonder if maybe we had the idea of who's the master in human/dog relationships upside down the whole time.

As with so many simple and profound things, Buddha said it best:

Master your senses,
What you taste and smell,
What you see, what you hear.
In all things be a master of what you
Do and say and think. Be free.

Dogs may not speak and, let's face it, they certainly lack the most discerning taste buds in the animal kingdom (we'll leave that to the finicky feline set), but they are forever demonstrating mastery over their senses. Sure their keen noses can dig up the ripe old bone they buried under your favorite rosebush a year and a half ago, but they can also smell out sincerity and kindness in humans.

And once we get over where their noses have been, dogs show us how to sniff out the best in ourselves. They use their finely honed sense of smell in miraculous ways, from warning families about fires in the middle of the night to locating cancerous moles in people, using their uncannily accurate muzzles to avert tragedies that smoke alarms and trained medical professionals have been known to miss. And that same sensitivity smells out need in a person, when a friendly nuzzle or a silly lick on the cheek provides a welcome, loving touch of comic relief.

While their taste buds may not seem refined, they certainly have favorite snacks—a crunchy stick, yummy new Italian shoes, or, best yet, the delicious squash of their favorite tennis ball. And in their taste in people, they have their favorites, remembering some folks after years of not seeing them, or even traveling hundreds of miles to reunite with their beloved humans.

Dogs see us for who we are, or even more masterfully, they see us for who we can be. A dog's loyalty helps it cast a blind eye to the ugliness in people who mistreat him, seeing only the beauty within that person as he patiently waits for the better side to surface. If we're wise enough to take a good look into a dog's soulful mirrors, we'll see that love reflected right back at us.

We've all heard about a dog's sharp sense of hearing, seen his ears perk up, and wondered what it was he was listening to. Some secret dog radio station only canines can pick up? Stories perennially tell of hero dogs saving people, hearing cries of distress with an auditory power so finely tuned it could only be housed in their hearts. Of course they do have that selective hearing problem—somehow the words *get off* and *couch* don't seem to register the same way *walk* and *dinner* do—but, hey, a pup gets hungry being so devoted all day, and what better place to chomp on a bone than a comfy sofa?

When their humans get home, they'll sit and listen to a blow-by-blow of everything that happened at the office, stifling yawns, never once making someone feel like there's something else they'd rather be doing. If you're thinking now, Who talks to their dogs?, as far as I can tell, the answer is simple—pretty much everyone. And why not? Who else listens like that? Dogs will always give you a fair hearing, presuming you actually *are* innocent. Even if proven guilty, your dog will never let on that he's on to you.

In a truly Zen fashion, dogs embody a level of fidelity, constancy, and steadfastness toward their people that Zen students usually can only aspire to reach towards their masters. Dogs show us what an altruistic nature looks like; help us shed our bonds of self-absorption and egotism to jump to the heights of devoted commitment, where we can learn to finally sit; and stay, firmly committed to our spiritual ideas. We can all take a lesson in nonjudgment from our four-legged buddies, who never judge us by the clothes we wear, the job we have, or the company we keep. They treat all people with the same generosity of spirit, ever re-earning their title of man's best friend.

Zen Dog was born of a desire to present pure, unadulterated dog love. Not only saccharine sweet, they're-sooooo-cute dogs, but the real McCoy kind of dogs, being Zen in the way only they can. We hope that, if only for a few moments, this book, more than just a tribute to furry little Zen Masters, will help us all take a good look at ourselves, through the mirror of the honesty, loyalty, devotion, and doggone pure spirits of dogs. When I meet a dog clearly present in her dogness, I always look her right in the eye and ask the same question, So, what do you do for a living? Inevitably any dog worth her Milkbones has the same answer, I'm just a dog. And simply by putting all her heart into doing what she came here to do, to serve her people, to teach us what unconditional love really looks like, to give us the present of learning to be present, she's done her dog job, like a true master. It is, after all, the readiness of the mind that is wisdom. One look at Rover's gaze fixed on your sandwich and you know he's ready and wise to the fact that if he gets the poor-pitiful-starving-me look down just right, you might succumb to those puppy-dog eyes. And if a crumb happens to fall in the forest of your living room, you know that your pooch's Zen mind will have caught it, for before the rain stops he can hear a bird. Even under the heavy snow he sees snowdrops and some new growth. Even under the couch, he can find those crumbs.

Thinking is more
interesting
than knowing,
but less interesting
than looking.

GOETHE/

THE LITTLE ZEN COMPANION

Just stay at the center
of the circle,
and let all things take
their course.

LAO TZU/TAO TE CHING

Do not think you will necessarily be aware of your own enlightenment.

BUDDHA / DHAMMAPADA

It is right in your face.

This moment

the whole thing

is handed to you.

LAO TZU/TAO TE CHING

Realize that we are not alone,

that we never have been

and never will be alone.

SRI DAYA MATA /

ENTER THE QUIET HEART

What is the sound of one hand clapping?

A SAYING DERIVED FROM A KOAN
BY JAPANESE ZEN MASTER HAKUIN (1686–1769)

Have the fearless attitude

of a hero

and the loving heart

of a child.

ANCIENT SANSKRIT MANUSCRIPT/

ZEN FLESH, ZEN BONES

Where can I find a man
who has forgotten words
so I can have
a word with him?

THE LITTLE ZEN COMPANION

The master acts without doing anything

and teaches without saying anything.

Things arise and she lets them come;

things disappear and she lets them go.

She has but doesn't possess,

acts but doesn't expect.

When her work is done, she forgets it.

That is why it lasts forever.

LAO TZU / TAO TE CHING

The sound of water
says what I think.

LAO TZU/TAO TE CHING

Look lovingly on some object.

Do not go on to another object.

Here in the middle of this object

lies the blessing.

ANCIENT SANSKRIT MANUSCRIPT/

ZEN FLESH, ZEN BONES

The fool who knows he is a fool

is that much wiser.

The fool who thinks he is wise

is a fool indeed.

BUDDHA / DHAMMAPADA

Free from desire,

free from possessions,

free from the dark places

of the heart . . .

rejoicing greatly in his freedom.

BUDDHA / DHAMMAPADA

The Tao gives birth to all beings,

nourishes them, maintains them,

cares for them, protects them,

takes them back to itself,

creating without possessing,

acting without expecting,

guiding without interfering.

LAO TZU / TAO TE CHING

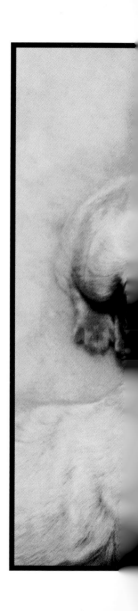

Everything the same, everything distinct.

Know the white,

yet keep to the black.

Be a pattern for the world,

the Tao will be strong inside you

and there will be nothing

you can't do.

LAO TZU/TAO TE CHING

What is your original face,

the one you had

before your parents

were born?

THE LITTLE ZEN COMPANION

Two mirrors
reflect each other.

A ZEN FOREST / 365 ZEN

Scratch first,
itch later.

ZEN SAYING

We are what we think,

all that arises from our thoughts.

With our thoughts we make the world.

Speak or act with a pure mind

and happiness will follow you

as your shadow, unshakable.

BUDDHA / DHAMMAPADA

Everything in moderation,

including moderation.

BUDDHA / *BUDDHA'S LITTLE*
INSTRUCTION BOOK

Feel the consciousness of each person

as your own consciousness.

So, leaving aside concern for self,

become each being.

ANCIENT SANSKRIT MANUSCRIPT/

ZEN FLESH, ZEN BONES

That little tail
is a strange thing.

GATELESS GATE/
ZEN FLESH, ZEN BONES

However young,

the seeker who sets out upon the way

shines bright over the world.

In him there is no yesterday,

no tomorrow,

no today.

Possessing nothing, wanting nothing,

he is full of power.

BUDDHA / DHAMMAPADA

The moon's the same old moon,

the flowers are just as they were,

yet now I am

the thingness of things.

BUDDHA / DHAMMAPADA

Lightning flashes,

sparks shower.

In the blink of your eyes,

you have missed seeing.

ANCIENT SANSKRIT MANUSCRIPT/

ZEN FLESH, ZEN BONES

Mastering others
is strength,
mastering yourself
is true power.

LAO TZU/TAO TE CHING

Your work is to
discover your work
and then with all
your heart to give
yourself to it.

BUDDHA / DHAMMAPADA

What is
the color of wind?

ZEN SAYING

When vividly aware

through some particular sense,

keep in the awareness.

ANCIENT SANSKRIT MANUSCRIPT/

ZEN FLESH, ZEN BONES

He who knows others

is wise;

he who knows himself

is enlightened.

LAO TZU/TAO TE CHING

I don't get tired of you.

Don't grow weary of being

compassionate toward me.

RUMI / *THE ESSENTIAL RUMI*

Only a clear mind knows itself.

LIN CH'AUN/

THE POCKET ZEN READER

Understanding and love
are values
that transcend dogma.

THICH NHAT HANH/
BE STILL AND KNOW

When the question is common

the answer is also common.

When the question is sand in a bowl

of boiled rice

the answer is a stick in the soft mud.

GATELESS GATE/

ZEN FLESH, ZEN BONES

Togetherness arises
out of separateness.
To find togetherness,
begin with separateness.
In this way there can be both
togetherness and separateness.

BUDDHA/DHAMMAPADA

Roam about until exhausted

and then,

dropping to the ground,

in this dropping be whole.

ANCIENT SANSKRIT MANUSCRIPT/

ZEN FLESH, ZEN BONES

The master gives himself

to whatever the moment brings.

He doesn't think about

his actions,

they flow from

the core of his being.

BUDDHA/DHAMMAPADA

Things to do today:

exhale, inhale, exhale.

Ahhhh.

BUDDHA / BUDDHA'S LITTLE

INSTRUCTION BOOK

He who stands on tiptoe,

doesn't stand firm.

He who rushes ahead

doesn't go far.

LAO TZU/TAO TE CHING

The miracle is not to walk on water.

The miracle is to walk on the green earth,

dwelling deeply in the present moment

and feeling truly alive.

THICH NHAT HANH/
BE STILL AND KNOW

He had no address;

he lived in a ball of dust

playing with the universe.

ANCIENT SANSKRIT MANUSCRIPT/
ESSENTIAL ZEN

You ask what nirvana is.
I would answer:
a certain quality of mind.

DALAI LAMA

Sitting motionless,

nothing happening

spring coming

grass growing.

A ZEN FOREST/365 ZEN

Who makes a show of himself,

does not shine.

Who affirms himself, is not recognized.

Who shows off, has no credit.

Who brags, does not last long.

LAO TZU / TAO TE CHING

If you know the power
of a generous heart,
you will not let
a single meal pass
without giving to others.

BUDDHA / BUDDHA'S LITTLE

INSTRUCTION BOOK

Our Buddha nature is there
from the very beginning;
it is like the sun emerging
from behind clouds.

ZEN FLESH, ZEN BONES

If the traveler can find
a virtuous and wise companion,
let him go with him joyfully
and overcome the dangers
of the way.

BUDDHA/DHAMMAPADA

PHOTO CREDITS

I wish to thank all of the owners and their wonderful dogs I have met in my journey as a photographer. You have given so freely and enthusiastically of your time—spent many hours with me and driven many miles to meet me. I have loved your evident pride, your energy, and your insight. And, of course, the many laughs, licks, head tilts, and tail wags. My profound thanks to you and to your beloved dogs—those pictured in this book and those countless others who are not.

TONI TUCKER